Beachcombing

To Jim
in friendship
Clifton

Clifton King

Beachcombing

ISBN: 978-0-9786935-3-4

Library of Congress Control Number: 2016904468

Cover design by author
Interior digital art by author

A few of these poems were first published, some in
different versions, in the following publications:
San Diego Poetry Annual, poetry organic.

Printed in the United States of America

Royale Road Publishing

for Katie Rose: my friend, my lover, my wife

I am happy anywhere I can see the ocean.
Anonymous

Contents

Beachcombing

An ebb tide leaves behind
those worthless passengers
of storm-tossed waves:
sinewy strands of seaweed,
shells and bits of driftwood.

I think of all I left behind.

I find a stone, smooth as a child's
face, flat as the earth before Aristotle.
I skip it across the shallows,
continue my search for something
I won't know until I see it.
That's the way of beachcombing
                              —and love.

Ashes
—for Jeff

Tomorrow, when I see the new blue
of morning sky, feel sun on my face,
I will think of you old friend,
all those hours we spent watching
the horizon, waiting on that perfect
wave, holding on to life.
And then breakfast at The Deli:
coffee, bacon and eggs seasoned
with stories of long ago travels;
afternoons in your living room,
dogs sprawled on the couch, and you
content in that canine clutter. But
your trips to the hospital scared the hell
out of me. How I admired your courage.
So tomorrow, when I see that new
morning sky, feel the sun's warmth,
I will think of those last minutes
I spent with you old friend:
that day in La Jolla Cove when we
let you go, a swirl of ashes, a spirit
who couldn't wait to return to the sea.

A Morning at Ponto Beach

Pelicans sprawl across a blue collage
of sky: a lazy line unlike those sharp
vees of migrating ducks and geese.

They dip low over the sea, mirrored
in her glassy surface, wing in unison,
then glide—wing, glide—wing, glide.

I wonder if the last in line
calls out the rhythm, the pace,
like a coxswain in a racing shell.

I listen, hear only silence,
that occasional surrender of waves.

Now, the pelicans are gone,
disappeared from sight in the time
it took me to write these few lines,

much the way life slips away
while we are busy with something else.

Office

My office has a window that welcomes
the ocean breeze, and at night, when traffic
on 101 has died down, that song of waves
finding a cobbled shore waltzes in. I have
a swivel chair like a government official,
an in and out box filled with papers
that are neither coming nor going.
On my desk, a pair of carved horse head
book ends that were my mother's favorites.
But why does someone who is retired
have an office you might ask. Because,
every man needs a place to do business.
Mine is the business of poetry.
And let's not mistake *doing business*
with *making a living*. Poetry pays only
in the self-satisfaction of words on a page,
in that polite applause after reading
to a room of fellow poets who are only there
for the open mic. True, I don't really need
an office to write poetry. Yet, I need someplace
for that four drawer file cabinet where I keep
all those poetry magazine rejection letters.

Coming Home

I was born on a beach
just beyond the reach
of high tide. Yet,
I have not always been
a neighbor of the sea.
In those years that survived
my youth, mountains,
the color of freedom, bled rivers
into the valleys of my dreams.
And the same rain that fell
on ancient conifer forests
nourished the Oregon lifestyle.
But, I was born on a beach
and have returned like
a spawning salmon
to end where I began.

Black & White
—after photo art *See No. Hear No.* by Heather Middleton

I have known women like you
in bars, on street corners,
in cheap hotel rooms,

lips dark with rouge,
pouting
like Marilyn or Brigitte.

You're all the same:
What's your name?
Who do you want me to be?

I have known women like you
with painted faces, and bodies
I spent nights trying to memorize,

breasts bound
by the black lace
of my fantasies.

I have known women like you
and have always wanted
to ask about the tattoos.

My God woman,
what
were you thinking?

I have known women like you
who would not listen,
who could not see,

so spent their nights,
wasted their lives,
with men like me.

Response to William Carlos Williams

This Is Just To Say

I have eaten
the plums
that were in
the icebox

and which
you were probably
saving
for breakfast

Forgive me
they were delicious
so sweet
and so cold   William Carlos Williams

I Must Say

I am disturbed
by the thought
of eating plums
kept in an icebox

as the flesh
of fresh fruit
should
tease the tongue

like
that warm welcome
of a woman's
mouth   Clifton King

7

How to Make Blackberry Wine
— a proven Oregon recipe

Get up early and make coffee.
Watch the sun come up over the Cascades.
This will not improve the wine in any way
but is a proper beginning for the day.

Have breakfast before setting out
to harvest blackberries. They are not
difficult to find along old fence lines,
perimeters of farm fields
and I know there's a big patch
behind the barn on the Wilson farm.
Beware of thorns and yellow jackets.

When your bucket is full, fingers
a brilliant purple from berry juice,
the harvest is done. Wash the dust
from your berries with the garden hose.
Pour them into a crock. Mash well.
Add boiling water, sugar and yeast.
Cover with cheesecloth
to keep out the fruit flies.

Later, when the time is right, siphon
into bottles (swallow a mouthful
now and then), cork and seal. But now
you must wait. Wine making is a slow
process and won't tolerate being rushed,
much like making love.
                    Think of this as foreplay.

Your Name

I spend the morning
at our beach
where the sky
is a collage
of confused clouds,
the ocean dappled
with only a thought
of whitecaps,
and a breeze
that whispers
your name.

Ashes of Life
after the California wildfires

The sea, calm as a sleeping child,
mirrors the skimming glide of pelicans.
A gull's cry pierces morning air
and I'm lost in the sun's warmth.

Offshore, a lone lobster boat.
A man on deck checks his catch.
I cannot see his face but know his
disappointment with each empty trap.
It has not been a good season.

Beyond the boat, a horizon tinted
with a brown ghost of smoke
from wildfires, those hazy remains
of scrub pine, willows and eucalyptus;
ranch style homes and barns, stables
and corrals, small summer cottages
and weekend shacks; everything
those flames exhaled
        after taking in all there was.

The lobster boat moves on.
And somewhere, in distant canyons,
along lonely ridges,
people sift through the ashes of life.

Needs

I cannot exist on words alone.
I need a bright morning
with a sliver of late moon,
sun rising yellow, setting orange;
butterfly wings, hummingbird beaks;
daffodils, dusty miller blossoms.

I need a sky clear blue, cloudy gray,
mid-day blaze of white, shadows
under foot; palm fronds
for an island hut roof; an old
pair of shoes; a new dog.

I need the sea, calm and glassy,
windswept and rough; nights
bedazzled with neon and starlight.

I need the touch of a woman,
the love of a woman.

I need you.

Poetry Book

It took years to compile these pages,
each word selected one at a time,
like Juan Valdez harvesting coffee beans.
It seems I did little else during those years.
Maybe that explains why my high school
sweetheart is now my ex-wife—maybe not.

Regardless of the cost, I have a book
of poetry. One might think fame and fortune
are in the near future. But, poets are a strange lot
unlike novelists and others who pen prose.
Poets must die, preferably by their own hand,
before fame finds them.

It took years to compile these pages. Yet who
will read them? Who buys poetry books?
In the bookstore customers will slide my book
from the shelf, browse its pages, then wedge me
back between all the other not-yet-dead poets.

It took years to compile these pages. If I had spent
that time on Wall Street learning the ins and outs
of hedge funds I could be driving a Rolls,
playing golf at the country club, living high
                    off other people's life savings.
But, I chose the road less traveled.
Say......that's a good line.

A Woman's Eyes

Brown dominates worldwide, blue second.
My mother's eyes were blue; a blue
that could make a summer sky jealous.
I wonder my father's thoughts
when he first gazed into her eyes?

And there are large round brown eyes,
like those you find south of the border:
pleading eyes of hungry children, knowing
eyes of their mothers. And almond shaped eyes
like those of ancient Egyptian women who
accompanied the Pharaohs into the next world.

A woman's eyes are a mystery not easily solved.
And often, one glance is all it takes for a man
to make a complete fool of himself.

Steve

His name is still in my contacts list,
his website still bookmarked
on my computer. Copies of *Lurid
Confessions, The First Noble Truth*
and *The Dumbbell Nebula* rest
on my bookshelf. I pull them
down, begin to read each again.
I first search out poems
I actually heard him read.
That way his voice comes back
to me: strong, able to reach
every crevice of a room
without a mic; his perfectly
timed pauses; the occasional
aside right in the middle of a poem.
Of course it's not the same
                —and never will be.

Steve Kowit 1938-2015

14

We Were There

We were there in The Haight, flowers in our hair,
beads around our neck; doe-eyed girls bared their breasts,
brandished bras; boys, not yet men, burned draft cards,
numbers in the devil's lottery, political punishment
                                    for being born.
We were there when napalm obliterated human decency,
burned babies in their mother's arms, denied innocence
                                    to those still in the womb.
We were there to see the oxidized eyes of dead come home
in boxes draped in broken promises; to hear dirges sung
like lullabies, lyrics that languished, lost graveside,
names resurrected decades later, etched on the headstone
                                    of history.
We were there, but turned away from that pile of bones,
left our failures to rot in rice paddies,
                    in undefeated jungles.
We were there that Friday in Dallas, heard the shots,
saw everything, saw nothing, watched a nation's dreams
                    explode, puddle on the hot pavement.
We were there when chants rose like prayers
into the Memphis air, black and white brothers at last,
brothers at last, then the angry retort of smoke and lead.
                                    Martin dead.
We were there at Kent State. Protest. Nixon. Cambodia.
Open fire. Fight back with your books.

We were there. We survived.
          Today, we think the same thoughts of the soul.

Street People

Set your clocks ahead, he says with authority.
I thought it was back, questions a guy
wearing tattered levis, two hoody sweatshirts.
(I seriously doubt either owns a clock.)
A third man shuffles up and sits down,
an old guitar slung on his shoulder.
He begins to strum, bob his head,
eyes closed as if in prayer. The air
filled with his homegrown rendition
of some sixties classic I can't quite place.
The others join in, hands clapping,
fingers snapping as Mr. Guitar sings
that fifties country song *Tom Dooley.*
I've always wondered what happened
to the Kingston Trio. They're alive
and well, living on the streets of Oceanside.
A fourth guy, stocking cap pulled
down over his brow, eyes barely visible,
stops to listen and joins in. Foot tapping,
he sings backup for Mr. Guitar
who has drifted into *Tell Me Why.*
Right before my eyes the Kingston Trio
morphs into the Four Freshman.
As the jam session winds down
Mr. Hoody Sweatshirts bums a smoke
from Mr. Stocking Cap and the inane
chatter of men with terminal sunburn
and shoes held together with duct tape begins.
Mr. Guitar produces a joint with the fanfare
of a magician pulling a rabbit from a hat.
It's passed around as eagerly as a hooker
at a bachelor party. The jam session begins
anew with even more creativity and gusto.

These men are living in the moment
and for a short time I'm a little jealous.
I never sang back up in a street band.
No stranger ever offered me a toke.
But then, tonight I won't be sleeping
under a cardboard box in some alley either.

Last Will & Testament

To my children:

I will leave nothing
I will take it all with me
I will take man's inhumanity to man
I will take terrorism, war, and those who wage it
I will take greed, stupidity, insensitivity
I will take politicians, liars, cheats
I will take hunger, poverty, illiteracy
I will take murder, rape, incest
I will take tyranny, bigotry, cruelty
I will take cancer, aids, every affliction known
I will take what was left to me—with me

Color

Blackbird fly, Blackbird fly
Into the light of the dark black night.
The Beatles

She was a girl I could have loved:
slender and dark, eyes the color
of a moonless night.

But, it was 1962 and there were
some things society didn't want
a couple like us to do.

Father took me aside and said,
Son, life is like a painting. Select
colors for your canvas carefully.

I told him I wanted the world
to see her color, each brush stroke,
every swirl of the palette knife.

Still, in my heart I knew there were
some things society didn't want
a couple like us to do.

It was a November night when she
came to me, tearful and trembling,
to say she was going away.

She was a girl I could have loved.
But my blackbird took flight,
lost forever to that dark black night.

Quake

Suddenly, the house moves beneath me,
a rhythmic roll like a mother rocking her baby.
The walls emit a low moan.

I recall the quake of '59,
that day I spent with Linda Parnell.
How we ditched classes, drove to Long Beach,
walked the pier, bummed smokes from fishermen,
watched palms quiver in a clear California sky
as a five-point-five rolled through. Later, we found
our way to Signal Hill, parked in the dark,
groped and fumbled our way into teenage love
in the back seat of my '47 Chevy.

The house twitches again. The fish tank
sloshes onto the kitchen counter. Goldfish
swim in circles, sense something awry.
A door opens itself with an *Inner Sanctum*
creak. That painting in the den hangs crooked,
threatens to spill a mountain lake onto the carpet.

Outside, streetlights sway, shadows
chase each other across the pavement.
I stand under a darkening sky.
Clouds steal the moonlight,
remind me how some things just slip away;
remind me of that night she left.
The radio announces a five-point-nine
centered somewhere near Borrego Springs.
I know there will be aftershocks for days.
Yet, I am unsure if she will ever come back.

Alabama Dawn

If I could write music
I'd write a song about an Alabama dawn.
I'd sing about swamp mist,
white as angels wings; morning dew
so soft it surely falls from heaven.

I'd sing about red clay hills
the longleaf pine, coal mines,
summer rain and Gulf Shore shrimp boats.

I'd sing about towns and cities:
Birmingham, Montgomery and Harper Hill,
Sealy Springs and Selma.

I'd sing about freedom riders,
freedom marchers,
freedom fighters
—if I was sure what to say.

I'd sing about the people:
innocent children, the old men
and women who know the truth.

I'd sing about the faces:
brown, black, white;
how they'd all get along
when they heard my song.

I'd sing about cotton fields,
Rosa Parks' bus ride,
drinking fountains,
segregation and integration
—if I was sure what to say.

If I could write music
I'd write a song about an Alabama dawn.

The Nature of Love

I recall those hours
we first roamed free
in the valleys,
across the plateaus
of our bodies;
how we pushed
against each other
like continental plates
that birth earthquakes
and tsunamis.

I can still hear
those small sounds
that flew
from your mouth
like hummingbirds
and hovered
in candlelit bedroom air,
spirits of our love affair.

Monday Morning

I stand at the coffee maker
sleep still heavy in my eyes,
tufts of hair shoot off
toward all points of the compass.
That old Ralph Lauren tee-shirt
she tried to toss a dozen times,
ragged around my neck, hangs
loose off my shoulders. This
breaks my pledge not to wander
the house mornings in only
boxers and a tee-shirt,
my promise to be properly dressed
and groomed before making
my morning appearance.
I hear her footfalls down
the hall: hard soled shoes,
not the padding of naked feet
nor the scuff of sloppy slippers.
She is a vision of morning beauty:
golden ringlets of hair bounce
with the energy of her walk;
a brilliant smile, lip gloss the perfect shade;
her skin vibrant with the secrets
of a Greek goddess; and those eyes
that smiled, no, laughed their way
into my heart. And the wrapping
on the package: a blouse crisp
in virginal white with just the right
number of buttons left undone;
black yoga pants curvy and clinging.
Good morning, she says,
her voice music to my ears.
Any plans for the day, she asks.
And just like that, I have one.
I want to keep her here
            —and mess her up.

Woodworking

My father was a self-proclaimed *Average Joe*:
a farm boy who joined the Navy, fought in a war,
lived to tell about it, got a job, bought a house
and raised a family. He was a homebody, didn't play
golf on the weekends, cards on Wednesday nights
or stop for a beer after work. What he did was woodworking.

Well, the truth is, he loved the idea of woodworking
but had little experience. Nevertheless, as soon as he could,
he bought the home woodworker's dream machine:
a Shop Smith. It transformed into a dozen different tools
that cut, drilled, sanded, shaved, mitered and sliced
any piece of lumber you threw across it.

My father's intention: make furniture.
A monumental undertaking considering the amount of wood
he destroyed under the saw. But, my mother humored him
and squeezed out a few extra dollars each payday
for the purchase of sacrificial lumber. My sisters and I
were often shanghaied to assist in different
phases of backyard furniture making.

But one particular Saturday afternoon my father
made it clear I was the chosen one, handed me
a sanding block wrapped in a fresh piece of 80 grit.
Both sides and all the edges, smooth, he said.
I stared at a large slab of plywood with curved sides
and rounded corners.

What is it? I asked. He said it was the top to a table
he was building for our neighbor, Miles Wilson.
So why doesn't he come over and sand it? I thought,
but held my tongue. Father checked on me now and then,
praised my work, then said, *Give it two coats of white paint.*
I spent the entire afternoon on that project, but soon forgot
about it with my birthday only three days away.

24

We had a family party. My big present was a basketball.
I wanted to go shoot hoops at the school. My father insisted
we play in the yard. *We don't have a basket*, I complained.
My father opened our back door. I stepped out into the yard.
There, perched on the garage, a brilliant white backboard
with a bright orange hoop complete with net. It was perfect.
Then it hit me: the curved sides, those rounded corners,
smooth edges and that white paint. My basketball backboard
bore an uncanny resemblance to Miles Wilson's table top.
I looked at my father. He was already laughing.

Sunday Ride

When you ride a motorcycle
it's not important the roads you travel
lead to where you are going.

The back road to Laguna Beach
snakes through Silverado Canyon
where clusters of small cabins
cling to hillsides, hidden
by a camouflage of trees and shadow.
You carve your way down the valley,
attack each turn, lean deep, defy gravity
and common sense. Your foot pegs
leave long scars in the pavement.
That staccato rasp of straight pipes
hangs in the air as you dash
through tunnels of shade,
flash across plateaus of sunlight.
Then, just as sudden as death itself,
clouds erase the sky and rain falls.
That double yellow becomes slick
as a used car salesman. Raindrops
sting like gravel tossed from heaven.
You creep into Laguna Beach,
find a Laundromat, strip down
to your boxers. There you stand,
a skinny, shivering, seventeen-year-old,
wondering what might happen
should someone come in to do laundry.

Our Beach

A white belly of moon lingers
in the morning sky, the only
blemish on that pale blue abyss.
A sandpiper's scurry catches my eye,
that race to forage before the next
surge of sea. Above me gulls circle,
call the ocean by name. Sun warms
my shoulders, throws my shadow
down the beach. I hear your voice
in the song of waves, recall that day
you wrote my name in the sand.

Aloha

We came home with tall tales
of the North Shore of Oahu:
Pipeline, Sunset Beach, Waimea Bay.
Wide-eyed surfers believed every word

about the North Shore of Oahu,
seldom surfed in those early days.
Wide eyed surfers believed every word
about that far-away, unattainable Mecca.

Seldom surfed in those early days,
those old style logs not up to the task
in that far-away, unattainable Mecca.
Hawaii beckoned, Barbers Pt. to Diamond Head.

Those old style logs not up to the task
at Pipeline, Sunset Beach, Waimea Bay.
Hawaii beckoned, Barbers Pt. to Diamond Head
and we came home with tall tales.

Afternoon Sidewalk

The sidewalk is crowded
with the usual characters:
tattooed men, (old enough
to be husbands & fathers)
who roll around town
like school boys
on their skateboards;
& those women, taut & tan,
determined to hold on to youth;
& the others, already round
with age & neglect;
& the old men
who sit on concrete benches
with their lap dogs
& watch the young girls.
Though you are nowhere in sight
this afternoon sidewalk will help me
get through the day.
But, without you,
how will I survive the night?

13 rue Paul Albert

The Eiffel Tower blazes like a torch
in these last minutes of a Parisian night.
Our plane touches down as dawn
spills across the French countryside.
We wander the airport, find our way
to the train station and into Paris.
Our apartment, a two-hundred-year-old
building, hugs a cobble-stone street
at the foot of Basilica Sacré-Coeur.
We find a bottle of wine, some fruit
and cheese on the kitchen counter,
compliments of the owner, an artist
who lives on the floor above us.
Sunlight slips through an open window
along with morning sounds of Montmartre,
the smell of warm croissants and strong
coffee from a little café below. We don't
bother to unpack but fumble with buttons
and zippers, litter the floor with clothing,
can't wait to be in love in Paris.

The Gift

I brought you a gift that morning:
two shells I found while walking
that beach we both know,
that beach awash in memories.
But, I forgot to offer them
as we talked and shared
small pieces of our lives
across that breakfast table.
I believe it was the contentment
in your eyes, in your voice,
the first time since he left.
So let me tell you of their beauty.
The first has delicate ridges fanning out
like a sunburst, making me wonder
if it exploded into creation.
It is delicately thin, nearly translucent,
mottled with the browns and bronze
of the sea. The second is thick, heavy,
with subtle, circular lines of color
like the strata of an ancient rock formation.
I wish you could see them,
beautiful in their complex simplicity,
much like our friendship.

Watercolor

A watercolor hangs on the gallery wall.
Liquid sunlight falls through
frenzied palm fronds. Dappled shadows
creep across white cabanas.
I want to know what those men
on the beach are looking at,
where they are going.
I imagine myself in the painting,
feel coarse sand beneath my feet,
midday sun hot on my shoulders.
Out beyond small breakers
a woman struggles
in the deep blue of depression,
her cries muted by mouthfuls
of sea green. I hear God's name
in her pleading, in panic that will
not keep her afloat. Has she
changed her mind about drowning
her failures. And who is that man
in the blue shirt, her lover, a friend?
I have the perfect place for this piece.
But, will I hang only the rustle of palms,
skies filled with threatening clouds,
men out for a walk on the beach?
Or, am I going to hear that woman's
cries every time I step into the room?

Black on the Boulevard

A serpentine line of bodies
stretches along the boulevard.
People standing shoulder to shoulder
in the rain,
in their convictions,
in a vigil for peace.

Their attire predominantly black,
the color of death
and mourning.
Someone has to wear black
until every single soldier comes back.

If only it were that simple.

There are no posters,
no chants of, *Hell no, we won't go.*
This isn't Berkeley in '65,
Chicago in '68,
and this isn't Kent State.
It's President's Day, 2015.

My God, we haven't learned a thing.

Risk

the risk we take is life itself
we have no choice in it
   thrust upon us while we are
   too young to object

but once we know
   once it is clear we are here
   to stay
   for that nano second of eternity

we must decide
   do I risk more than just being
   do I risk having thoughts of my own
   do I risk living life as God intended

          risk being a wife   mother
                  husband   father
                          friend
do I risk speaking out
risk the criticism
risk putting myself out there
                to be an artist   a creator

        painter   poet   photographer
                  writer   sculptor

do I dare
how can I not
this is who I am   why I am here

Shooting Rabbits in the Mojave

On a night so dark it almost hurts
your eyes to look at the stars, we walk
alongside Danny's truck somewhere
in the Mojave Desert, headlights ablaze,
like soldiers on a search and destroy mission.

For some reason, jackrabbits gravitate
to headlights like moths to a flame.
So, rifles ready, we wait for their dash
down that tunnel of light
           — then blow them all to hell.

Being city kids we don't know a barrel
from a butt when it comes to guns. More
than once a rifle raised to kill a rabbit finds
a friend in the sights. But, the dumb luck
of youth is with us. We survive the night.

We never hunt rabbits again. Mike enlists,
goes to Vietnam. Danny and I go to college.
Then, the telegram. I've often wondered
if it was just Mike's destiny, or did he use up all
his luck that night shooting rabbits in the Mojave?

Yard Sale

The morning air holds traces of last night's rain.
But the yard sale has been planned for weeks.
You can't back out now. You've already called off
too much in your life. So you display your collection
of unwanted memories on an old card table,
along the edges of the driveway, on the lawn:
that German knife set, a wedding gift from your
first marriage, their handles a dark tight grained
wood, blades forged from the finest steel, sharp
as that line that separates sea from sky; the odd
assembly of cups, bowls and glasses whose mates
long since lay shattered on the kitchen floor
courtesy of your loser ex-boyfriend. He's gone
now, after years of holding your heart hostage.
The red bulbous body of a leaf blower hunkers
down on the drive its long black snout pointed
skyward, a snake of cord tangled around itself.
Does it work, asks a young man, his black lab
tugging at its leash. You should have at least
wiped off the dust, tried for a few dollars more.
You search for an outlet, plug it in, male into female.
The switch won't budge. It purrs like a small kitten,
not the roar of a lion. The young man leaves
without a word. Maybe you can fix it you think.
But then, you couldn't fix your first marriage,
or your second, so you do what you've always done:
toss it in the trash.

Thursday Morning Thoughts

Through my open door I look down our street
toward the Pacific, slender palms stark against
a cloudless morning sky, that faux horizon
of red tile rooftops of multi-million-dollar
homes. I hear waves attacking the bluffs
along Carlsbad Boulevard, that occasional
train whistle, Marine helicopters cruising
the coast serious about their war games.
My second cup of coffee sits on the desk,
steam rising from that dark elixir
the way I imagine magic vapors materialized
from Aladdin's lamp. I take a sip, make a wish.

Fog begins to roll in. Sandburg wrote:
it comes on little cat feet. This fog muscles
its way ashore like a bull. Damp air edges
its way through the door, the way an open
refrigerator spills cold onto the floor.

I'm reminded of motorcycle rides in the fog:
the early sixties in Seal Beach, a summer's
evening ride south along PCH to Huntington,
or inland to visit a girl I knew in Buena Park.
I'd fly along wrapped in the comfort of youth,
nothing more than a tee shirt and Levi's
to shield me from the night. Fog lay in hollows,
in open spaces that have long since disappeared.
It reached out, grabbed hold until my bones rattled.

Now, I sip my coffee, notice the fog has lifted.
That's life along the coast, life everywhere:
look away for a minute—everything changes.

Secondhand Heart

She gives me
a secondhand heart
she found lying around:
one of those
tiny candy hearts.
Its message reads,
I love you.
But, I wonder
who was
the original *you*?
And is the same true
of a secondhand heart
as that of a secondhand car:
you're just getting
someone else's heartaches?
Yet, I accept this small,
somewhat suspect,
pink token of her love
and pop it into my mouth,
but find the sentiment
hard to swallow.

With You

You open to me
as a morning glory
obeys the rising sun
and I know
how God must have felt
the first time He heard
His name offered up
in prayer.

And though
I have become
one of those old men
who, like my father,
can't imagine
where the years
have gone,
I know where
and with whom
I want to spend
those I have left.

Apps

I don't own a smart phone.
Don't have an app
to help me find a place to eat
then post a picture
of my meal on Facebook.
Don't have an app that tells me
the freeway is gridlocked,
commuters on the brink of road rage,
their Starbucks Mocha *whatever*
gone cold in biodegradable cups,
some considering suicide by collision.
Don't have an app that reveals
how far I've walked or exactly
where I am on that worldwide grid
of latitude and longitude.
Don't have an app that allows me
to watch movies on a four inch screen,
or one that lets me kill space aliens
while I wait for a green light.
And because I don't own a smart phone,
some suggest I live in a cave. Maybe.
But in my cave: a novel or two,
a stack of poetry books, inked words
emblazoned on real paper
waiting for that slow turn of the page
               —no apps necessary.

Demise of a Delphinium

Blossoms litter the ground,
leaves limp as the proverbial
wet dishrag. She has but one choice,
ruthless as it may seem to some:
amputate stems with those pruners
she had sharpened just last week;
rip roots, still searching for that moisture
of life, from the earth. Toss the remains
into the greens bin. There they mingle
with others of a similar fate, to be
mulched and laid to rest in flowerbeds
at city park playgrounds where children
run and laugh, unaware of death's proximity.

My Daughter's Cats...

climb and claw their way
up the easy chair,
like Sir Edmund Hillary
up Everest.

But, once on the summit
the cats curl up and nap:
no flag to plant,
no photos to snap.

A Drive Down PCH

I crest a gentle rise in the road
and the Pacific greets me
with a blue I've never seen before.
I turn onto Pacific Coast Highway.
My tires slap over each expansion
joint of this old concrete slab roadway.
I'm reminded of days when this
was the only link between San Diego
and my boyhood home in Long Beach.
I recall the overwhelming fragrance
of flower fields, that pungent aroma
of rotting kelp in the summer sun,
this same cadence of tires on concrete.
Carlsbad State Beach, perched atop
an ever eroding bluff, hugs the highway.
Sinewy coastal shrubs, bent from
the weight of a relentless ocean breeze,
separate campsites. How different
from the Oregon coast where I spent
the seventies and eighties. There,
mountains of old growth fir crawl along
the coastline like a spinney-backed serpent;
the Pacific boils out of control,
not surrendering to breakwaters and jetties
like those that overpower the California coast.
Road noise changes. I realize I've driven past
the beach where I'm to meet my sisters.
I glance at the small silver box on the seat,
Well, they can't start without us can they Dad?

Winter Beach

This winter beach mimics
summer. I'm unable to ignore
those women, lithe and lovely,
lying on warm sand, unafraid
to expose pale winter flesh,
flat bellies of youth, thighs
and shoulders smothered
with sunscreen. But soon,
like chameleons that cling
to a setting sun, skin turns
pink, then scarlet, as they
sacrifice themselves for a tan
that will seduce any man.
I consider calling, ask if
you've been outside,
try to decide how to broach
the subject of my interest
       in your tan lines.

Saturday Thoughts

I slip into an old sweatshirt, faded shorts;
grab a thermos of coffee, my notebook
and wander off to my favorite beach bench.
The sidewalk is still damp with last night's
rain. Those purple florets along the bluff
cradle tiny droplets in their petals.
Silver clouds sweep in off the ocean.
On the sand a man and young boy toss
a Frisbee. I watch it float between them,
recall a summer Sunday in '74, three friends,
iced beer in a cooler, a Frisbee marathon
that lasted well into evening.
Has it really been forty plus years?
In distant gray waters a dolphin surfaces,
blows a ghost of breath that lingers in still
air, the only evidence it was ever there.
The horizon is being swallowed by fog.
The air chills, becomes thick in my lungs.
I am drowning in thoughts of youth and age.
An old man shuffles past, his small Terrier
wearing a sweater. Three women strut by
in time to some silent aerobic mantra,
firm bodies displayed in tight shorts, brief tops.
He doesn't give them a glance. My mind
reels with fantasies and I fear that day
when small dogs replace women.

Vigilante Gardeners

A woven wooden trellis
alive with roses
stands between us
and our neighbor's yard:
a jungle of dandelions
and crabgrass,
a constant threat
to our potted geraniums,
the chives and basil
we water
with the lead free hose,
our miniature peach tree
that yields only
two or three globes a season.

She is a practicing recluse
venturing out only
on Wednesdays
to attend mass,
receive communion.
So we wait, listen
for the rattle of her old Buick
as she leaves for Saint Patrick's;
arm ourselves
with spade and sprayer;
sneak into her yard,
attack and kill
every broadleaf in sight.

Paris Hat

She bought it in Hawaii
with France in mind.

Now it sits in her closet,
doesn't go with her blouse.

I'll take a scarf, she says.
Paris nights can be cold.

So, that hat planned for Paris
is now her latest pool wear.

I only hope she doesn't
change her mind about men
like she does hats.

Watching the Last Sunset of the Year

Wind blusters down from the north
where foothills veiled in snow
glow under an early evening sun.
The dogs are busy in the brush
doing what dogs do when unleashed.
In the campground across the highway
motor homes and tents perch atop
a bluff overlooking the Pacific.
The sun drops lower in the sky,
a glorious display of red and apricot.
Everything in silhouette, dark
against dying embers of another year.
I wonder, *How many more?*
But of course, we never know.
I call the dogs and head home
to love my woman as if it were
our last time—our first time.

Reflections

after *A View of Lake Casitas,*
watercolor by Courtney Strand

We see you meandering through
greens and purples, nestled in
steep valleys. Your arms reach
into the back country, strangle
oak and alder—everything
below your high water line.

We remember a time before
you suffocated these valleys
and meadows: the Chumash, *
caretakers of this land for millennia;
Coyote Creek alive with cutthroat
and salmon; wild with winter runoff,
elusive in the heat of summer;
small farms and large families,
hopes of the future planted
in rocky soil, watered with faith.

And we remember your creation,
the damn that birthed you,
chaos of construction, the blasting,
a forest uprooted, earth ripped open
only to receive itself regurgitated
from diesel giants, again and again,
until you spilled over—our savior
with your sacrament of water.

Yes, we see your placid waters,
pastel hues of sky and hillsides;
a scene so serene we nearly forget
those life and death struggles.
But in our hearts are memories
your reflections do not reveal.

* The **Chumash** are a Native American people who historically
  inhabited the central and southern coastal regions of California.

Another Day at the Office

It's been years since that clutter of desk,
inane babble around the coffee pot
in a windowless tomb of capitalism.

Now, my office is the edge of the sea,
sand warm beneath bare feet. No one
to meet except the incoming tide.

On the sand, remnants of the weekend:
plastic pails, Tupperware tubs
and towering turrets of sandcastles.

I park along the curb where rusted relics
of Detroit iron regurgitate a semi-melodic
ruckus; where tattooed young men

and guys gray with time gather
for our morning ritual in the waves.
Just another day at the office.

The Parking Job

Her car teeters on the precipice.
Tires cling as if glued
to the edge of our concrete drive.
I fear gravity & the super moon
may pull her into that quagmire
of sandy soil & ground cover
that creeps along the block wall.
But I wait until after breakfast,
after eggs & fresh cantaloupe,
toast with orange marmalade.
I hold my tongue while coffee
brews, fills the room with
its delicious aroma. Then I speak
in a voice as loving as possible,
You almost missed the driveway.
The instant these words fall
from my lips I know I've misspoken
and attempt to turn it into humor
with an uncomfortable laugh.
Later, I call the insurance company,
double our coverage.

Garage Sale

An old man, his truck jammed
with other people's castoffs,
haggles over the price of a used surfboard.
His skinny arms hang from a tank top
that hugs his scrawny body like the tees
worn by muscle builders on Venice Beach.
He is one of the serious scavengers,
people who cherish everyone else's junk.
They gather like fruit flies on an overripe
banana, hovering above the scraps of life.

Two women park their rusty Camry
on the wrong side of the street four feet
from the curb. They cruise the driveway
debris without a word, like searching
the ruins of a sunken pirate ship for treasure,
then head off down the street
still in search of that special something.
I don't understand the garage sale mindset,
that need for something you don't need.

Enough of that. I'm on my way to Costco
for a shaker of garlic salt. I can save
a-dollar-twenty if I buy a case of thirty-six.

Special Delivery

I almost sent you a Valentine's Day
card complete with little pink hearts,
angels, ribbons and red roses.
But, this is not a day for casual
comments about hugs and kisses.
And we are not school children
exchanging tokens of friendship,
every child assured their share.
No, this day is for lovers, those
serious about the sensations of body,
warming oils and candlelight;
for the man and woman
who dare to tangle afternoon sheets,
flesh still damp from the shower.
I would send one of those cards
if I thought it would satisfy,
make you to call out my name,
conjure up a quiver, induce a sigh.
But I have to say, I'd rather give it
to you personally. It's that kind of day.

Joy of Summer

I stop at my favorite café, order coffee and
wander out to a sidewalk table next to a group
of old surfers: guys with skin like leather from
years on the water, in the sun; guys wearing levis,
sweatshirts and flip flops just as they have for
decades. I settle in with a book I can't seem
to get into. They talk about swell direction,
argue whether Swami's or Trestles has the best right.
They laugh about John's old truck that threw a rod
on the way to Windansea, complain about
the new parking meters in Oceanside.
I sense a change in the chatter, peek over
my reading glasses to find a twenty-something
woman at their table. Long blond hair
falls down her smooth back. Her skin,
the color of sun mixed with beach sand,
luminescent with youth. This is the same
beach girl look I couldn't resist when I met you:
blond curls trying to escape from a sunhat,
the joy of summer painted on your face,
the rest of my life swimming in your eyes.

Invitation to a Bath Party

There is nothing more enchanting
than a woman fresh from a bath,
skin still damp beneath a wrap
of terrycloth; that faint fragrance
of body wash; those lingering beads
of water between her shoulder blades,
in the small of her back; strands
of wet hair clinging to her nape.

Bring bubble bath if you wish.
You may play with my rubber ducky.

Pleasure

This morning I find the word *pleasure* scribbled
on a piece of paper lying on my desk among the clutter
of coffee cups, a copy of Steve Kowit's new book
& a zip drive I had to have, but never use.
The word seems not to notice me. It just lies there:
pleasure, on a piece of 24 pound, bright white printer paper.
Pleasure, I say to myself. *Now what was I going to do
with this word? Is there a reason it's in caps?*
I sense myself developing Billy Collins tendencies,
the mundane becoming the focus of my life. I fear
I might go to the kitchen & write about salt & pepper shakers.
So I leave *pleasure* lying on my desk & try to forget it.
But I can't chase the thought of *pleasure* from my mind.
Pleasure—my first ride in a fast car or bending
a motorcycle around those blind curves on Signal Hill.
Pleasure—my first girlfriend, our first kiss;
fries & a cherry coke at Harvey's.
Pleasure—those easy high school days cruising
A&W, windows down, Chuck Berry cranked up.
Pleasure—your smile in the morning; that first cup of coffee,
cream & sugar, & don't tell me real men drink it black.
I look at that word lounging on my desk, know there was a
reason I wrote it down. But I also know my reason was lost
during the night. If only I had made a few notes.
Then I'd have a stanza or two to torment me,
                                    instead of this single *pleasure*.

After Labor Day

Summer lowers
into autumn
and September
surrounds us.
That flowing
sweep of sand
lies naked
as sand castles
and footprints
are erased
by the tide,
forgotten
by the hordes
of yesterday.
Gulls huddle
against the wind
while sandpipers
dance
near water's edge.
The pledge of fall
paints a purple sky
and once again
we are free to be
alone with friends.

Summary Steelhead
from the Oregon days

You find a small crescent of green earth cradled in a bend
of the Little Nestucca River. A place where sun reaches your
shoulders all day, where Douglas firs crowd down to water's
edge, road far enough away to be forgotten, yet close enough
to retrieve lunch. Here the ritual begins: lace eight pound test
though ceramic and wire guides, careful to caress each, like
laying on hands, asking the Gods for a good hunt; tie on a
snap swivel, bite off excess line with your teeth even though
you have a knife in your pocket; clip on a homemade Okie,
add a glob of salmon roe; drift and bounce your bait down
every riffle on this stretch of river; lose it again and again to
that rocky bottom. But, that's where you catch steelhead,
that's where you spend the hours. Yet, when you're alone in
the woods, wandering through lush meadow grass in search of
the perfect place to surrender to trees and sky, become a leaf
adrift on a cool stream, link your soul with mountain waters,
time is something best left behind. And when wading a small
stream, freshet filling it bank to bank, steelhead holding in the
shadows of the shallows, you think of nothing and everything,
ask questions, expect answers from a tangle of ferns along the
bank, from a slippery knot of roots, from that small patch of
blue sky that follows a morning shower. As shadows lengthen,
time, that you have tried to ignore, ticks away somewhere in
the distance. One last cast you tell yourself and plop an Okie
just downstream of a big boulder. Your line goes taut. The
silver back of a steelhead flashes, turns and runs downstream.
She lets the current work for her, pulling, pulling. You're
running out of line. You follow her: a step, reel in, a step, reel
in. You straddle a fallen tree, slip into water up to your knees.
Your line goes slack. You've lost her. Suddenly, that zip of
monofilament through water. She dashes toward the opposite
bank. You're tangled in a small branch, struggle to get free.
The Gods are watching, somehow, the line frees itself.

She is tiring. You wade after her. She lies on her side in six inches of water, looks up at you with one ebony eye. Overhead a red-tailed hawk circles. You kneel, hold the rod tip high, capture that thin translucent line with the fingers of your left hand. You imagine asparagus, a spinach salad on your dinner plate, taste that tang of fresh lemon squeezed over a steelhead fillet. She thrashes, makes a final lunge. At this instant, on the road behind you, a log truck rumbles past. Its engine rattles the afternoon air. Yet, as clearly as a mother hears her baby's cry in the night, you hear the line snap. Your steelhead floats upright, lies motionless on the gravel bottom, then darts into the current and disappears—
not unlike those forty years of your first marriage.

At the Airport

We watch people and wait
for the eight-twenty flight to Tucson.
Father comments on a girl nearby
with red streaks in her hair,
a small gold ring in her nose,
then, somehow segues into a story
about Mildred, the wife of a man
he served with aboard the USS Idaho.
My father, nearing ninety, has told all
his tales many times before and after
a few words I know the whole story,
but listen for those small changes
that come with advancing years.
Now boarding, they announce.
We say our goodbye. A flight attendant
wheels my father up the ramp,
around a corner and out of sight.
Should I have said more, given him
a bigger hug, kissed his face? Will I
look back on this day, wish I had?
Or will there be more visits, more
changes in the way he remembers life?

Old Man in the Mirror

He stares back from the bathroom mirror.
I'm startled at first, then, I recognize him:
hairline creeping back toward that
Gene Hackman look; gray at the temples,
like Cary Grant in his last few films;
small wrinkles around the eyes, some
sun spots, a bit of the Marlboro Man look
just like every other working class Joe
who made his living out in the cold bite
of winter, that oppressive heat of summer,
and yes, those wonderful spring days
when office guys dreamed at their windows.

I study the old man in the mirror, notice
he's getting a little thick around the middle.
When did that happen? I ask. He doesn't
answer. *You really should take better care
of yourself,* I say. He just stares back.

I mention an article in Esquire: *Being
a Better Man in 2016.* It's simple: eat less,
exercise more, cut down on dairy, salt
and trans fats. The old man just stares back.

I turn off the light, head for the kitchen,
grab a handful of chocolate chip cookies
and a glass of milk, flip on the TV and flop
into my recliner. Ah, a double episode
of America's Test Kitchen. I wonder if
that old guy in the mirror heard a word I said?

Rabbit Stew & Wild Mushrooms
— for Jerry

You always wore a grin, were easy with a laugh.
You claimed it took fewer facial muscles to smile
than frown. Not lazy, just looking for the easy way.
Yet, we didn't make it easy on ourselves those early years
when we terrorized woodshop together; were more than
disruptive in Biology. You grinned through it all while I
secretly worried about my GPA. Weekends we cruised
Harvey's, A&W and The Gut; smoked non-filter cigarettes;
drank beer from quart bottles; shouted obscenities at those
guys from Jordan High. And how many times did we bump
start your old Ford truck? I went to college, if you can count
driving by the campus on the way to the beach. You went to
work—now and then. I got married. The Army got you.
Years slipped by, almost unnoticed, consumed by the joys
and disappointments of life. But, our adolescent attitude
remained intact. We rode motorcycles up and down the Baja
peninsula; bought boats we couldn't afford; repeatedly
rejected membership in adulthood. The sixties left in
shambles, we moved our families to the great northwest.
You grew a beard, I tried. You built a house in the woods.
I lived in town. We rode dirt bikes in the forest, over towering
coastal dunes; fished for steelhead in the Little Nestucca;
poached spring Chinook in Cedar Creek. We ate rabbits you
raised out back, and mushrooms gathered in the Tillamook
mist. Our children picked blackberries, caught poison oak
together. And, looking back I realize those were the years
our wives began planning their escape. Through the eighties
your marriage dissolved. You moved in with *the other woman*.
I returned to California like a salmon drawn back to its birth
place. A decade later that devil divorce visited my doorstep.
We lost touch after decades of thumbing our noses at society.

Then, last December you drove down from Oregon to visit
your late brother's wife. I could see the years on your face,
but insisted, *Jerry, you're looking good.* I think we both knew
you weren't. We talked about everything and everyone
that afternoon of memories. You're my best friend, yet,
I don't remember ever telling you so. Maybe men don't.
Sunday we talked again, in the shade of that old maple.
Your headstone leans a little. Most people wouldn't notice,
but I did and mentioned it. I know you laughed at that.

Tired

I'm tired of the rush for things
that don't really matter, for things
important to other people.
I'm tired of the lack of respect,
not for me, but for all mankind.
I'm tired of the weak and poor
being used to make the rich, richer.
I'm tired of the drive away from where
I want to be, to where I have to be.
I'm tired of bad air, ignorance,
the traffic, the threat of stupidity,
Fox News and those who believe
                everything they hear.
I'm tired of waiting for people to change,
for the light to change, for the other guy
                to make up his mind.
I'm tired of success being measured
by the make of your car, the number
of bathrooms in your house, or how rude
you can be and get away with it.
I'm tired of things that aren't going to change
                and things that have.

The Clubhouse

For two boys of twelve it was a grand plan,
a dream as enormous as Noah's ark.
So, he became our inspiration.
For if one man could build a boat big
enough for all those animals, certainly
two kids could construct a simple clubhouse.
We had the perfect location behind
my garage where an old duck pen stood.
The duck had belonged to my sister.
Both were gone. The duck ended up
in the oven, my sister in Seattle.
But where did Noah get building materials?
Did they come with God's command
to construct the ark, like a kit, instructions
and materials included? Or did Noah pray,
then find a stack of lumber
in his front yard the next day?
Since we were under no such command
from God, and being devout Catholic boys,
we prayed. We prayed for 2x4s and plywood,
we prayed for corrugated tin roofing,
we prayed for a solid wood door with a window,
we prayed for a box of nails.
But when morning's light brought neither nails nor
wood, we waited for the dark of night, then swiped
what we needed from a nearby construction site.
It was the summer of '55. James Dean died
alone on a lonely road. The Brooklyn Dodgers
defeated the New York Yankees in the world series.
And we spent the warm summer nights in our new
clubhouse dreaming about Mary Lou and Virginia,
the two girls who lived on the next street.
For two boys of twelve it was a grand plan.

Blind Love

I was sighted once, knew the time
of day by the color of the sky;
the seasons by the direction
of waves. But, I was not in love.

I could assess a woman's beauty
from across the street, judge her
by the curve of leg, swing
of hips, the shape of her smile.

The rest of the world made little sense:
trees and money that same green;
moon and sun like balls of yarn
in Aunt Sara's knitting basket.

Then, you stole my sight, struck
me blind with a single smile.
Now, my hands see the small
of your back; line of thigh to knee.

My mouth has visions of your lips,
soft flesh of neck and shoulders.
And that fragrance of your hair, damp
from a bath makes me, what's the word?

Intoxicated—yes, that's the word.
But, *drunk*—that's the truth.

The Porch

I bought this house for the porch,
open to the west toward the Pacific.
Ocean breezes curl above the railing
and nudge our windbell into song.
This neighborhood is a bit older
than I'd like. (But then, so am I.)
Evenings I wrap myself in the quiet,
a security blanket worn thin by the years.
This old porch is more than concrete
and wood, brick and mortar.
This porch is a day at the beach,
a night in the desert, an afternoon
in a lover's bed. It's a trip down PCH
in that fast lane of my youth, the first
girl I kissed, that day I filed for divorce.
This porch is the morning my mother
died, our Paris apartment, that train
trip we didn't take to England.
It's the evening my daughter was born,
my first and last day of college,
all those skipped classes in between.
This old porch is our day in Central Park,
Strawberry Fields and Yoko's apartment.
It's Monet's lily pond, my bronzed
baby shoe perched on the bookcase,
our wedding day. This old porch
is that Harley I rode too fast, the first
time I held my granddaughter,
the last time I saw my father.
This old porch is you and me
together in that warm wind of life
       flying our love like a kite.

Father's Hands

I look in the mirror and see my father.
(I think it's the eyes.) I hear his voice,
feel the touch of his strong hands.
He always worked with his hands:
a Kansas farm boy milking cows, planting,
harvesting wheat, mending fences; then,
the CCC road crew before joining the Navy
to fight for his country, his hands loading
shells into the deck cannons of the USS Idaho;
and thirty years as a milkman who never
missed a day's work, raised three children,
and loved the same woman for sixty-eight years.
I'll never forget Father's hands; hands
that worked and fought for me, cared for me,
hands that helped me though life.

Prayers of a Friend

A man can have no better friend
than one who keeps him in her prayers

I look into the face of God,
like many people, when I discover
there is no one else who can help,

when the numbers are against me,
when those in the know don't know,
when all I can think of is family.

I look into the face of God,
expect Him to ask my name
since we haven't talked that often.

But He knows me like a hummingbird
knows a honeysuckle; the horizon
the sun's touch; like I know you.

I look into the face of God
believe miracles happen in the Bible
not on the streets of California.

But then He speaks, as He must have
to Moses. His voice every thunderclap
ever heard, every baby's first cry.

I look into the face of God,
like many do, when I discover
there is no one else who can help.

He says, *I shall answer this prayer.*
But Lord, I haven't asked yet.
I know, He says, *but someone else has.*

Writing a Poem for You

I take my coffee to the porch,
look out over red tile rooftops
bright in this pale dawn light;
distant palms, subtle curved lines
in the morning sky. An ocean breeze
turns our flowerbed into a ballet.
Roses bow their heads, French lavender
sways while those yellow blossoms
of a dusty miller look on.
I hear the neighbor's fountain gurgle
in those silent moments between
that far off call of a crow
and a mocking bird's mating song.
I imagined I would write a poem for you,
here on our porch, you tending
to flowers, me with pen and paper.
But, I've come to realize it's not where
the poet writes that births a poem,
rather, where the heart is. Mine, my love,
is with you, and you are my poem.

Bridge

I stand atop a new bridge on PCH:
curved steel and concrete arch,
form that flows like the steam below,
the sea that rushes toward it.

That old bridge, really nothing
more than a fancy box culvert,
began to slip into the sea,
sag under the burden of time.
Built back in '27: the same year
Lindbergh soloed to Paris,
The Jazz Singer made movie history,
the year my father lost his father.

I imagine those bridge builders
as they labored with the weight
of wooden forms; concrete
mixed on site, one part cement,
two parts sand and aggregate,
an untold amount of sweat.
I can hear them now as they talk
of how the world had changed:
movies that speak, flights across
the Atlantic. Yet, not a word
about my grandfather's death.

So I speak my father's name,
this year of a new bridge,
this year of his death,
so that all might know him
should he pass this way again.

New York Heat

I recall the first time
we kissed goodnight
then awoke
in the same bed:
that small hotel room
in Greenwich Village
with its faux fireplace,
red velvet wallpaper
and those ridiculous
steer horns on the wall.
Outside, people scurried
along the sidewalk,
a heated chorus of taxi horns
threatened pedestrians
and echoed down
a tree lined canyon
of old brick façades.
You slid closer.
We found each other
between the sheets.
We missed breakfast,
and lunch. All the while
that window air conditioner
labored to save us
from spontaneous combustion.

Wanting You

Sometimes, when my heart aches
I climb that bluff along
Coast Highway, watch the sea,
in whatever mood she might be,
toss waves against shore, white
foam smeared across the sand
        like frosting on a cake.

This morning her waters inky
gray mirror clouds dark enough
to pass as an Oregon sky.
And always the gulls,
        their incessant pleading.

True, there was another
that held my heart for decades
in that mechanical clatter
of pistons and valves; under
the spell of two wheels balanced
between exhilaration and disaster.

At night I dreamt of speed,
blind corners on forest roads,
those last few feet of an unconquered
hillside. But those were years
of a young man unconcerned,
oblivious to his own mortality.

I cannot recall what happened,
which paramour I chased so long
before that time. But now,
well into my seventh decade,
all I want is the sea and a woman.

Interested?

Running in the Yard

Today, my childhood home
looks much the same as I remember
even though its rough stucco exterior
is a different color and that old acacia,
that dropped yellow blossoms like
a snow storm, is gone. And that jungle
of ivy that consumed the entire corner
of our front lawn is now just a memory.
In the back, a room has been added
where two orange trees stood. A Valencia
and a navel: juice for breakfast,
orange boats for school lunch bags.
The rest of the backyard is that same
patch of grass surrounded by planters
built by my father with homemade bricks.
Yet, it seemed larger when I was a boy
tossing a football or playing with our dog.
I remember my father and me
having footraces in that yard.
I never lost a race and couldn't
understand why he was so slow.
Years later I had a son of my own. We ran
across that same lawn, and I understood.
It's love that makes a father slow.

Writing a Love Poem

I tried to write you a love poem.
I looked up exotic sounding Italian words,
a few French phrases, thumbed through
a thesaurus until my fingers turned blue.
I almost fell back on those old standbys:
firm fleshed thighs and star bright eyes,
recounting the pleasures of being with you.
But I wanted something more than just
verbal lust. So I stepped outside to beg the stars
help. They sent words crafted from light;
dazzle plucked from that blanket of night;
chants used by the ancients, tossed into a fire,
hammered on anvils of passion and desire.
Yet, pagan songs and foreign foolishness fail
to convey what I really want to say.
Be Mine sounds so simplistic. Honestly,
I tried to write you a love poem.

Unarmed

police have murdered
another child of color
high school student
unarmed high school student
unarmed child of color
murdered by police

police officers
trained in techniques
to subdue a suspect
trained with night sticks
trained with pepper spray
trained with a taser
yet, they chose bullets

we did not hear the shots
we did not see the child fall
unarmed high school student
unarmed child of color

only police know
only the child knows
unarmed child
unarmed child of color
murdered by police

and, he is not alone
in that graveyard
of the unarmed
the names are as many
as a mother's tears
as many as her cries of grief

Dyzhawn Perkins   19-years-old
Tony Robins Jr.   19-years-old
Michael Brown Jr.   18-years-old
Tamir Rice   12-years-old

unarmed children
unarmed children of color
murdered by police

no indictments
no trials
no justice

no tomorrows
for those children of color
unarmed children of color
murdered by police

Extraction

The dog and I sit on the porch.
He is stretched out, taking it easy,
as if he put in a hard day at the office.
For me the pain medicine isn't working,
so I pop another. My body knows,
down to the very marrow of my bones,
that a small piece of the whole is missing.
The blood is a protest, my mouth in mourning.
The pain relief is too subtle. I pop another
pill, drift back to the morning's ordeal.

The dentist puts her knee on my chest
like a narc who has just taken down a junkie.
Small grunts leak from behind her mask.
Beads of sweat dot her forehead.
I wonder if she regrets choosing
dental school over Harvard Law.
On the tray next to my chair
every stainless steel instrument
found in a B movie torture chamber.
You will feel nothing, she says. The pressure,
like a small truck running over your jaw,
is normal. That cracking sound, similar
to a glacier calving, is normal.
You will feel nothing, she says.
Her assistant holds my shoulders
against the chair. The Dentist has
both knees on my chest now. Then,
my tooth, rooted like a white oak
for six decades, finally surrenders.

Back on the porch, afternoon sun
warms my face. An ocean breeze
rattles fronds on my neighbor's palm tree
and the pain medicine has kicked in
like a runaway locomotive.
An egret wings its way in the distance,
Janis Joplin astride its back. My dog
levitates up and over the porch rail,
disappears in a flash of light.
The potted geraniums sing
Lucy in the Sky with Diamonds.

And, as promised, I feel nothing.

Faith

Go home and write
A page tonight.
And let it come out of you—
Then, it will be true.
Langston Hughes
Theme for English B

Write a page, then, it will be true.
If only I could believe
the way Lazarus believed
the words of Jesus.
If only my words were as compelling,
this page as powerful.
If only I could believe
I would write my mother—alive.

Yet, we all know real truth
reveals itself in the rewrite.
So I would edit her last two weeks
before the Doctor's words, sharp
as a scalpel, surgically removed
every speck of hope—
Brain cancer. Inoperable.

Write a page, then, it will be true.
If only I could believe
I would rewrite my father's despair,
construct a sentence, or paragraph
that would recover this last decade
lost to loneliness and grief.

For my sister I would erase that playful
utterance to her children forty years ago,
Let's have a picnic on the lawn.
Maybe then, her two-year-old son
wouldn't run into the yard, into the street
where he is struck and killed by a car.

And for my children, and their children,
I would pen a future of fortune
and good health.

Write a page, then, it will be true.
If only I could believe.
Would I revise myself, those early years,
change a day or a decade knowing
my new path may not bring me here?

Write a page, then, it will be true.
If only I could believe.
But, my words are not the words of Jesus,
this page not the word of God.
I am but a poet.
Yet, for a moment, for a stanza or two,
life would be as I wrote it,
if only I could believe.

Exquisite

When I think of *exquisite,* I think of women:
long legs, slender hips, Audrey Hepburn neck,
a walk that says, *look at me, but don't stare.*
Yet when I think of the beach, *exquisite*
isn't the first word that comes to mind,
until I remember a line in a poem I read:
...exquisite as a day at the beach.
Then, images of deserted sand castles,
cloudless skies filled with the cry of gulls,
footprints in wet sand left by lovers with
no destination beyond each other,
that insistent surge of sea, cold swirl
of ocean around your ankles, warm
beach sand beneath a blanket, sun
bright on your face and body as you
offer them up to the tanning God,
give me reason to reconsider.
Long legged women, with their wonderful
walk; a day at the beach. Yes, exquisite.

To My Children

Someday, my children, after
my final breath, after I've
watched my last wave
roll up this cobbled beach
I hope they find me
slumped in a patio chair,
sun on my face, coffee
cup on the table beside me.
But then, we really don't
have a say in the end.
(Although many poets have
chosen their own hand.)

Someday my children,
when personal possessions
are gathered, that final
business of death, don't
expect hidden bank accounts
or extensive real estate holdings.
And there will be no small
steel box stuffed with cash,
all certainly squandered by then.
What's left you'll find scattered
about my desk, those pieces of life
too valuable to hide away:
pictures of family and friends
—and my poetry.

Royale Road Publishing

Made in the USA
San Bernardino, CA
19 April 2016